# Lions At The Gate

*To: Bonnie;*
*God Bless*

Poems by C.L. Carey

*Charles L. Carey*
*Feb. 11 2011*

authorHOUSE

*AuthorHouse™*
*1663 Liberty Drive*
*Bloomington, IN 47403*
*www.authorhouse.com*
*Phone: 1-800-839-8640*

© *2010 C.L. Carey. All rights reserved.*

*No part of this book may be reproduced, stored in a retrieval system, or transmitted by any means without the written permission of the author.*

*First published by AuthorHouse 3/2/2010*

*ISBN: 978-1-4490-7610-8 (sc)*

*Library of Congress Control Number: 2010900467*

*Printed in the United States of America*
*Bloomington, Indiana*

*This book is printed on acid-free paper.*

*For God, Lena Carey, Kathryn Wilson, and all of my friends that cared enough about my writing—thank you.*

## About the Author

*I write to obtain a taste, a taste of poetry, a taste
of passion and, a taste of the world.*

*Also the ability to write something about that taste, until the sweet
taste of love is in my mouth, for the people in this world.*

# Table of Contents

## I. Inspiration

The Bench .................................................................... 3

Honor In Grief ............................................................. 4

She Wore a Yellow Ribbon in Her Hair ...................... 5

A Soldier's Story ........................................................... 6

Fathers, Part I .............................................................. 8

Fathers, Part II ........................................................... 10

I Write to Obtain a Taste ........................................... 12

Take My Mind Beyond the Trees .............................. 13

Fireside Characters ..................................................... 15

One Beautiful Piece .................................................... 16

Two Tin Barrels, Part I .............................................. 18

Two Tin Barrels, Part II ............................................ 19

Dreams of the Night ................................................... 20

Sleeping Dragon Theory ............................................ 21

Mother ........................................................................ 22

A Little Playmate ....................................................... 23

Asleep in My Seclusion .............................................. 24

## II. Nature

Lilies of the Dance ...................................................... 27

The Winds ................................................................... 28

The One-eyed Cat ...................................................... 29

Ray of Gold ................................................................. 30

A Hummingbird's Song .............................................. 31

A Snowy Wonderland ................................................. 32

Today ........................................................................... 33

Her World, Mother Nature ........................................ 34

The Mountain So Still ................................................ 35

The Mountain ............................................................. 36

Caspian Sea ................................................................. 37

The Grasshopper..................................................38
A Mountain, She Cries.........................................39
Down By the Sea..................................................40
The Sea Within the Trees.....................................41
Indigo Bunting ...................................................42

## III. Mystery and Romance

A Serenade of Love...............................................45
The Scary Prairie..................................................46
The Game .............................................................47
Down the Darkened Road that Calls the Night ....48
The Deep Well Summons Her Today....................49
Time Will Tell ......................................................50
Gone, Just Gone ...................................................51
An Article of Death ..............................................52
Oh My Marie, Part I.............................................53
Oh My Marie, Part II ...........................................54
Echoes in the Galleys............................................55
My Certainty—Love ............................................56
Shanties Down By the Railroad Tracks ................57
Mercy On Me .......................................................58
Oh What a Web She Spins ...................................59
Savannah ..............................................................60
Young Love, Part I.................................................61
One More Night With You ...................................62
We Only Have Today............................................63
Torn at the Seams .................................................64
Warriors of the Night............................................65
Blind Fears ...........................................................66
An Enchanted Night ............................................67

## IV. Religion

Hungered Thy Flesh..............................................71

Angels Among Us ................................................................72

The Rock of Time ...............................................................73

Destroying the King ...........................................................74

The Hunter .........................................................................76

Innocent To Death ..............................................................77

A Kid's Prayer to God .........................................................78

Confessions of a Soul .........................................................79

Yes I Can .............................................................................80

The Pricelessness of Life .....................................................81

# I.

## *Inspiration*

# The Bench

As I sit here and there, alone in my despair
with no one to care
through winds that roar,
through hardships of rain and snowy nights
beyond the sorrow and beneath the troubled plight—
who will sit on my bench today,
who will call life my way?

A comforter of sadness
for the distressed and those who fear
truth and conviction as they stop and stare—
just a bench that truly cares.

For those in need of me,
I'll be there through fallen tears
laughtered moments—my secrets are dear.

Under the cold, beneath the frost
secrets are told.
Mysteries so gallant, they do unfold.
Mysteries of life somehow bought and sold.

For who hears the ringing of the church bells—
I, who hears the silence of the night alone.
For I am the bench of life for the young and old.

## Honor In Grief

Behold the mighty reapers story told
    beyond the tears, beyond the years
Through time ye must fade, a heart, a soul.

One step beneath the valley of the dark
    saddened tears in a quiet park.
One trumpet sounds through war and death
    tumble flashes up through a mind
    memories do withstand all tests of time.
Shattered feelings shake and roar
    within oneself a closed door.
Saluted by honor one mournful flag flies
    fallen to a war's lonely cries.

Through time everlasting shall be no more
    parted from life, one widow's war.

## She Wore a Yellow Ribbon in Her Hair

She wore a yellow ribbon in her hair,
a soldier's widow, to show she cares.
Her memories last through and through
Her tears fall down from a war so cruel.
She wore a yellow ribbon in her hair—
Oh who wouldn't stop and stare?
Beneath the meadows, beneath the air,
She wore a yellow ribbon in her hair.

# A Soldier's Story

As a child my dreams are caring and free,
with emotions of a childish play.
Although learning who I'm to be
with choices, with the realms of a new day.
Gallant decisions of who Life
will allow me to become,
within the freedom, within this
land of true liberty and justice for all.

A young man, a father, and a native son
awaken to a soldier fighting to be me,
from back roads, city streets, and mountains so high
the who, the what, the reasons why.
For my oath to be a soldier
within the red, the white, the blue
for me and you.

As God took his precious hand and
watched over me, beyond
the mighty seas.
Through the hardships of the midnight air,
with frightened silence, one lonely flare,
beneath the stars
with the proud and the few.

For we as soldiers,
carry the battles from year to year,
through bravery and fear,
through silent moments alone and afar,
with gallant tears that crumble
like an earthquake in time.

Standing for freedom
through the stripes and the stars,
with weeping tears that fall silently
within my mind.
Battles will be lost and come undone
with wasted lives beneath a saddened sun.

Beneath the rainy nights and cold
winds that blow,
comforted by each other
with laughtered moments
from a reflective rainbow.
For who will Gabriel's silent horn
call through our troubled plight?
Yet another battle and another flight.
Through peaceful mountains, quiet valleys
and shattered hills, blood-trodden reflection
and broken wills.

Standing on a hope and our commitment
to make all men and women free,
through blood, sweat, and tears, and our free society.
We march on through hardships and pain,
through heated anger and saddened rains,
above the victories and though they came,
through unripe vineyards that make no sound.

Many souls lay in wait, one man down
beneath the foliage, a hidden fear lies low
frantic quietness in the morning cold.
Through fields of darkness and ungodly sights,
he lies with anticipation through his own troubled plight.
As the guns rattle through the mystic pain,
we are soldiers, that's our claim to fame.

*Lions At The Gate* | 7

## Fathers, Part J

Humble beneath so many shattered dreams,
that do fall short of fortune and fame.
Burdened with success, throughout silent shadows,
beneath hidden fragments and through silent rains.
Tainted joys that fall beneath seedless soils,
that bear forsaken fruits from a withered vine.

Cuddled laughter that shakes a weary soul,
through tears that grapple with one's bountiful harvest
that gives some truth within the pride
and worthiness from a girl or boy.

Standing within the true victories for which they bring
beyond an unworthy world and yet
bound to their glory or failure, to thee we sing.
Gone towards wayward dreams
that gather their silent praise.

Beneath joyful laughter, beyond
the stillness of so many days.
Through unforeseen that rob us
from true success as a Father.
They rip through our pride and
shatter our emotions with
weeping tears that never fall to the ground.

Through truth and conviction
that must not be ignored,
for they are guided by the Heavenly Father,
to which we all owe anything and everything we do.

Though we assemble our families
that will carry the burdens, hardships,
vain choices and decisions of Fortune or Fame,
through many restless days, troubled plights
many journeys and sleepless nights.

We as fathers will withstand all tests of time
and weather many turbulent storms
that our children will put us through.
But we will stand firm and give our wisdom,
joy, tears, cherished moments that give us great pleasure
to see them at moments that they become
Mothers and Fathers.

## Fathers, Part II

Though failure, success, gains, profits, and losses
seem to be the daily grind,
and we slowly lose our children with time,
we must understand that our Heavenly Father
is also watching over us.
Though we obtain more and lose less
within his precious eyes,
with our needs, wants, desires, dangerous pleasure and greed.
So we press on through the daily grind, slowly
losing fragments of our mind,
but we press on and on.
Through some of us have kept
our promise to him up above,
through our true desire to keep him first,
and never last.
We stand strong and proud with the true sincerity
to help other fathers that somehow have lost their focus
and the only true way to the kingdom
that is at hand.
Save our children, for they are worth saving!
For our Heavenly Father gave his only begotten son to save us,
who shed his precious blood on the cross for us.
There can be no greater sacrifice than this.
Though we somehow have conquered many obstacles
that life has presented to us as Fathers,
although we've bypassed many,
we somehow succeeded through our own understanding
that our Heavenly Father is still in charge.
Our daughters and sons have followed in our footsteps
to become prominent in society,
to which we claim no victory
but victory of truth, guidance,
true leadership with passion, perseverance
and joy of being a product
of our Fathers before us.

We stand in the midst of them to which
they pioneer for our greatness,
and true leadership.
We claim victory to nothing
but the simple qualities
that were passed down through them.
Many of us have searched
and prayed with sincere hearts
and truth and honor and forgiveness
of our own faults
for which there were few or many.
But we prevailed with discipline,
and sincerity and forgiveness
from our Father up above.
Motivation that all of these trials and errors
would lead to success,
which we as Fathers could accept
as our true products
of our own good deeds
for which our children have become
Doctors, Lawyers, Accountants
or many other professions.

# *I Write to Obtain a Taste*

I write to obtain a taste,
    a taste of poetry
    a taste of passion
    and a taste of the world.

    Also the ability to write
    something about that taste
    until the sweet taste of love is in my mouth.

    For the people in this world,
    I really need to learn patience.

    The Hunter hungered thy Flesh.

# Take My Mind Beyond the Trees

Where prairie dogs roam
Through mountain peaks and quiet streets
Across barren lands and hills of sand
Across hearts of stone and childless homes
Take my mind beyond the trees.

Between sunny days and subtle ways
Between gallant embraces and hilltop places
Beneath tearless smiles and enchanted isles
Beneath a blink of an eye
Beneath the blue in the sky
Take my mind beyond the trees.

Into the depths of the sea and what awaits for me
Into hurt, pain, and cleansing rain
Clasp the touches of no retreat and love sweet
Clasp the fruits of family and love
Take my mind beyond the trees.

Hold the breath of a child with no despair and rush forth like fresh air
Hold your heart within mine and taste the
sweetness as grapes on a vine
Touch the stars through your eyes at night and
sing melodies of a troubled plight
Touch a mind that dreams of gold and comfort for a weary soul
Take my mind beyond the trees.

Plant a seed that would forever grow and warm
the spirit from the midnight cold
Plant words of comfort and need, that would
silence hunger and selfish greed
Feel the heat of days gone by and never know the reason why
Feel the rain as it descends to the ground and
soar like an eagle without a sound
Creep through the imagination of time, for whatever rhyme or reason

Creep upon the moonlight lakes and rumble
the sound of an earthquake
Take my mind beyond the trees.

## Fireside Characters

Nowhere to go, nowhere to roam
nomads of a breed, without a true home.
Forsaken by hardships or a disease or two,
bewildered and stained by addiction
through and through,
with darkened clouds and never to be blue.
Castaways to no fortune nor fame
with barren nightmares beneath the darkened rains.
Twisted and dangled above the burning flames
of time gone astray, beyond the inner times.
Through broken tears that hide inner pain
creeping to a beat that never rhymes
chasing moments through a shattered hour glass
with hopeless sorrow from a weeping past.
Perceptive pleasure all ripe and torn
with broken battles from a piercing thorn.
Daunting through a road of lust and fear,
gamblers of a life so far and elusively clear.
Riddled through mystery, beneath a saddened sun,
shackled to a chain of fire
and a forever burn.

## *One Beautiful Piece*

Along the line of honor, pride,
creativity and childhood dreams,
bewildered by a silent breed,
yet words take shape through many forms.
Cultured and nourished fulfillment
are stretched into the seams
of a life to be.
Awakened by reality
through dawned passages of time
thoughtless clouds flow gently across a page,
beneath the crystal pain of desire.
For who would dare to compare the creative imagination
with words of hardship, hope, and despair.
Through gathered emotions fling and flow
beyond the silence of one's lonely chair,
could thy words romp and rage
with dashing wonder beneath the air
of a moment in time that must stand still?
Though tears and heartache need repair,
through wondrous words of a distant
reprieve, of a written verse or two.
Yet inner sadness retreats
for a moment in time.
Denounced childhood fantasies
not to be a pact
formed in deceptive rules
that govern a written way or form.
Passing through a freedom that changed
a melody of one's true heart.
Transforming a mind, through an impassive
thought, that reached higher to a level of success
though we are the poets, the dreamers,
and story-tellers at best.
Fighting beyond the realm that warms a fragile soul,
sanctioned to an order beneath a natural gift

that one must display,
yet humbled beneath the guidance
of a power beyond, a mightier way.
Though truth and fantasy roll of the mind
with gentle accord,
priceless expression knocks at a closed door.

## Two Tin Barrels, Part I

Two tin barrels in the frosty cold,
faded through time, many years old.
Gone to time so wasted and still,
weakened by sorrow, strengthened by will.
Through humble moments
in stormy rains,
through crumbled sadness
it weathers its pain.
Shattered echoes ring its retreat
beneath the shadowed streets.

# Two Tin Barrels, Part II

One barrel, two barrels,
    not three,
standing in painted moments
    so silent and free.

Standing beneath a destiny,
    within the alleys of fate,
thou quiet, bane, and desolate.

Beyond the distant reprieve,
    beneath a quiet light
through flashes that sparkle
    beyond a distant plight,
through winds that roar
    of a haunted night.

## Dreams of the Night

What happens to a dream
  that slowly slips into the light?
Does it warm the soul
  beneath a fallen night?
Can it last into the depths of one's
  troubled plight?
Carry a lonely teardrop beneath the air
  and raise the moon to a summer delight?
Upon a galaxy, upon a sparkle,
  beyond the midnight breeze and
  starlit wonders that lie so real,
  that quiets a mind through the trees.
Through the gentleness that will flow and touches
  one's true desire
  that only a dream will flow into the night
Through the journey flows into the passion of days so rare,
  with moments that are kindled there.
That weight into the night as it sleep
  repairs its hardship and pain.
Through the bitter tears that fall beyond
  the cleansing rain and yet dreams are so clear.
Rainbows shine into the echoes or time
  and distant journeys bring joy within a mind.
Memories so young and bold are lost to eternal cold,
  but still yearns there moments in time
  beyond the fragility of unspoken lines.
Dreams must fly into everlasting memories
that are meant for you and I.

## Sleeping Dragon Theory

Lurking in the cracks and crevices of one's soul,
hidden in the darkness and beneath the outer layers of life,
coupled with heartache, pain, and strife
his presence is gallant and bold.
Speechless in languages of near and afar,
deceptive moves beneath the stars.
Souls are of a dying breed,
honesty trapped beneath its greed,
a kiss or two, or maybe three.
Hopelessly chained beneath the sea,
piece by piece, for whatever price
deceptive pleasure, cold as ice.

## Mother

I watch her star from my window at night,
she brought me joy in the daylight.
I watch her smile with no compare,
her fragrance was like fresh air.
She sang melodies of wisdom, that was her fame.
She ran like horses, her spirit unclaimed.
Her love for children was at its best,
doing for others was her quest.
Kindness was her nature through and through.
Oh, who wouldn't dare to love her zeal
always truthful, always for real?
Never a teardrop from her face,
she had no color, she had no race.
She walked so proud, she walked so free,
She gave me love and joy,
she made a man out of me.

## A Little Playmate

Daddy's at work and mother's away,
big sister's heartbroken for one more day.
I play house alone to pass the time away,
building blocks or spelling in clay.

Mother says she's having a boy, a girl I pray,
riding on a big wagon all full of hay.
Summer's fun with no one to play,
how about little Linda or a little Kay?

## Asleep in My Seclusion

The world moves around my dim dark day,
within the loneliness, through words that stay.
Drifting upon a distant time,
upon a soaring turbulence
which carries me away.
Beyond a moment that is slow to pass
to a place that drips my hidden reflections
through a golden hourglass.
Above the fragile mist that lurks
beneath my wayward sea,
that ripples to my shoreless spree.
Distant memories dance through
my fluttered dreams which comfort
endless sleep in repair
through the windless air.
Frantic movements awaken my closed eyes
to a new day that dawns,
that somehow hides my memory
that drifted into the night.

# II.

## *Nature*

## Lilies of the Dance

Brightened fields upon the spree
stirrups clang the stately pace.
Fragrant honeysuckle beneath the tree,
busy little bees, like busy little bees.

Playful bunny, one summer's mate
Thunder chatters about the day with
clouds of concern in a darkened sky.

Lilies sway in their windy dance.
Peacocks flutter in their natural prance.
Willow trees fling their hair up high,
clouds bring forth the daily cry.

Misty rain flows to a stringed harp melody
Lilies of the field slumber to a degree.
Awakened crickets click and clack
Swans a swimming, in a pondly pack.

Night of armor blankets lilies' field,
silence so golden, silence so real.

## The Winds

I tried the gale winds
    that night
beneath the starlit
    light.
Came a prancing through
    my hair
and twisted my cap
    without a care.
Blew into my window
    with ease
as tin roofs flapped beneath
    the breeze.
Though clouds rushed
    their hurried pace
and autumn leaves swirled
    gracefully in place.
It ripped and roared the night
    away
as calmness came of a new
    day.

## The One-eyed Cat

Could she see one of me,
or does she see two of me
with that one eye.
What does a cat see with one eye?
Does she see alright or
all of the night?
I wondered why they called her one eye,
she seems so shy, never replies.
She runs with her bell, so I'll always tell.
She never had a name until I came,
that pretty little bell,
that pretty little bell,
until I met that gal.
Her colors are gray and black
that sweet little cat.
She's now my cat
and that is that.

## Ray of Gold

Upon a meadow, down by a
    quiet brook
beyond a dream within wayward
    castles afar.
With golden reflections that binds
    life to a distant star.
Subtle moments that glance throughout
    a silent book.
Golden touches, reaching out
    beyond a glance.
Bewildered through a separated affair,
    that came through a lonely place in time.
That flared beneath a wishful moment
    that came through
    an idle mind.
Casting a dark shadow that
    is never again
Forgiven through the passage
    denounced to man.

## A Hummingbird's Song

Gracefully dancing amidst the days
    so fair
beneath a rose petal, beneath the air.
Through time, beyond the sweet summer
    trees,
daunting and dashing through
    the gentle breeze
bouncing beneath the lilies of the
    day.
Through suckled pleasure of a distant
    way,
moment by moment with each taste full of
    desire,
minute by minute, hour by hour.
Through subtle reflections and
    beyond the fields of play.
As they swing and sway, through
    mountain's peaks
    and quiet streets
Through clouds of blue
    for you and me.

## A Snowy Wonderland

Graceful birds soar in their
    playful sway
upon a gentle breeze, upon the
    whitened trees.
Flakes of laughter dance beneath
    the chilly day
Chatter silenced to a
    moment in time,
as snow lifts wisps
    to a steady climb.
Sleigh bells ring on a galloping
    sleigh
as barnyard doves huddle with
    nothing to say.
Silent closeness begins
    to unfold
through hurried kisses
    in the frosty cold.
Playful squirrels glance
    with a watchful eye
as one lone predator
    glides across the snowy sky.

# Today

Today is the day
when all is fair
like flowers that sway
and love awaits there.
Across rainbows' light
that falls doomed to the night.
As cotton fields dress in flair
like mountain peaks that dance
in the barren street.

Today is the day
when summer breeze
flows quietly
through the blossomed trees.
As dandelions grow at bay
beneath the rolling thunder's cheer
that quickens in the attentive ear.

Today is the day
that passion flows in a golden stream,
a bounty harvest
within a dream
that awaits a moment
within a day.

## Her World, Mother Nature

She has impassioned us all
through her subtle touches
beyond the midnight clear.
Her impurity glows
through a piercing soul
and yet she weathers
a man's desire.
Her soul cries tears that flow
beneath the fury of a sea
but still she turns her head
in silence of a morning dew.
Her eyes sparkle through the stars
at night and blows the wind
beneath a windless kite.
Through brisk winters,
snowy peaks, quiet valleys beyond
the troubled streets,
she dances through wild winds
so graciously sweet.

## The Mountain So Still

Whirlwinds dance through the stillness
of his embraceable arms,
beneath its silence, beneath its charm.
Generations gone and yet to come,
only he stands as one.
A mountain of hope through hardship
and despair,
blanketed by heaven and earth
and one Mighty God to thee,
free from bondage and yet captured
by its beauty.
For who does the mountain call
beyond the echoes,
the valleys and the hills?
Oh what a thrill,
big brother to the raven, the hawk,
the bald eagles that soar.
Brother to the ocean and sister
to the quiet shores
with gentle reflection
through winter, summer,
and fall.
Rumbling thunder beyond the mighty call,
beneath trickling drops of rain
that fall so gallant and bold,
He gives life to life
and life to death
that can't be bought or sold.

# The Mountain

Caressed by her blanket
of soft mist and dew,
he lies asleep,
beyond a hidden view.
Cuddled by his mother's
loving arm, embraced by
the mighty oak and pine,
braced by strength and wisdom
beneath a gentle mind.
Thou winters so crisp, yet
warm and still.
Never weeping his silent zeal
beyond the valleys, beneath the hills.
Through tunneled passages
beneath a wayward sea
crumbled and pulled beneath
a silent greed.
Plunged into a day
all ripped and torn,
still weathered and warm,
beyond tomorrows
and yesterdays gone.
Now weeping willows
show their love for him.
As time will be everlasting
and he shall be no more
beneath the hidden shadows
beyond the silent wars.

## Caspian Sea

Oh Caspian Sea, Oh Caspian Sea,
things aren't what they used to be.
The mighty sturgeon's home, a way of the past,
black gold mines and hidden gas,
one slow life has come undone
separated into parts and never to be one.
Oh Caspian Sea, Oh Caspian Sea,
things aren't what they used to be.
Once ruled by giants and now by greed,
plenty for us, a poor man's need.
Oh Caspian Sea, Oh Caspian Sea,
my sea, my sea, my sea for me.
Oh Caspian Sea, Oh Caspian Sea,
things just aren't what they used to be.

## The Grasshopper

The grasshopper jumps here
    and there,
eats all day without a care,
sleeps at night until
    the morning dew
beneath the sky so blue.

The grasshopper hops here
    and there,
stares about without a care
    but flocks of sparrows! beware!
and toads hunger beyond the air.

The grasshopper still leaps here
    and there.

## A Mountain, She Cries

Below the heavens, she stands so tall and wide
through winds that roar and snowy nights,
with trees of wonder, from side to side.
Beneath her laughter and gentle streams
in the morning light.
Through quiet echoes beyond her troubled plight,
giant oaks fall to a world's needy delight,
with quiet tears and gentle fears
that yearn beyond a silent ear of time.
Vanished birds no longer within her loving arms,
gone are her everlasting memories
that chase her wondrous charm.
Thunder roars above her mighty call
but yet it trembles in the darkened halls.
Raindrops trickle down her shadowy peak
with barren memories
through distant streets.
Snowflakes fall upon her weakened soul
that dances beneath the frosty cold.
Songbirds sing beneath
her fruitful canopy that reaches
beyond a gentle sea.
Her silence is so golden and true
it touches a moment in time
through and through.
Reaching into a world so cruel and unfair
a dream so heavenly born and rare.

## Down By the Sea

Down by the sea,
           the sea,
                the sea.

By the sea,
          oh beautiful sea.

The sea that
    rushes
        forth
           to
         me.

Down by the sea that comforts me,
Down by the sea, so gallant and free.
By the sea, moonlit nights so starry.

Oh beautiful sea,
    the heaven, the earth, the sea
               and me.

## The Sea Within the Trees

Never seen the sea
    float through the trees
    the trees, the trees.
Never seen the sea
    flow beneath an oak tree.
could the sea be the sea?
    A tree just a tree,
    the sea, the sea?
Do the trees grow during the day
    or does it grow
    during the night
as the darkness sleeps beneath
    the twinkled starlight?
As the sea rips and roars, its frantic spills
    beyond dreams that flow
    upon quiet wills
    that lie silent and still.

## Indigo Bunting

Indigo bunting, why do you cry?
I've seen the lonely teardrop of
a mother's cry.
They stop and stare,
as if not to care.
I didn't know why
as they passed her by.

Indigo bunting, why do you cry?
I've seen the lonely teardrop
of a mother's cry.

Indigo bunting why do you cry?
I've seen the lonely teardrop
from a mother's child's sigh
I've seen the lonely tears fall
from a lonely mother's child
as her lonely mother sighed.

# III.

## Mystery and Romance

## A Serenade of Love

Within my silence, alone and still yearning
    to hold you tight,
beyond the innermost touches and
    through my everlasting desires.
Beneath a moment, beneath a darkened night,
    within the stillness that glows
    through my eternal fire.
Beyond a shallow stream, beneath the rumble
    of my roaring sea.
Before my sorrow, before my lonely tears
    that will fall,
through the stillness and through
    the enchanted halls.
Beyond quiet places near and far,
    beneath the Milky Way,
    caresses that only I decree
    beyond a fallen star.
Beneath my soul that awaits
    in  a silent galaxy.

## The Scary Prairie

Tumbleweeds scurry across barren plains
winds wisp through the valley so still
and wolves howl their nightly calls.
These predators dash and dart
through the canyon walls.
Falling stars disappear beyond
the distant way,
upon the distant hills.
Mystical imagination becomes so real,
wayward echoes alert weary minds
then slowly disappear
beneath the tranquil moon
with her watchful eye,
beyond the heavenly sky,
through the day that gives no reply.

## The Game

For who will play?
Memories that I've yet to forget.
Dreams of yesterday's past
and tomorrow
is in wait
of dawn's rise.

Of a new day.
Hearts grow fawned
like a pawn.
Who is yet to win the game?
And the Queen has gone
astray.

Can never be explained.
For who will say,
"It is only the game."

## Down the Darkened Road that Calls the Night

Saddened willow trees hang their hair
as fireflies sparkle their
elusive light.
Lonely owls echo beyond the chilled air.
The darkness glooms around
the covered moon,
as candle lights sway
and begin to appear, so clear.
Church bells ring a golden hour of time
beyond the playful desire's within
one's mind.
Barnyard doves, all quiet and still
behind the distant road, beyond the distant hills.
Predators of this darkened road are
assured of their frantic moves
as prey scurries beneath
the nightly dew.

# The Deep Well Summons Her Today

Whose laughter went unseen
as her lonely tears fell.
The child stopped to sit a spell
as the deep well called out
her name.
The stone dropped
from her tiny hand
and the rippled waves
gave no reply.
Reflections glowed
from a mirrored stand
with illusive pictures
in a distant sky.
Little stones could not compare
to haunted memories
so deep there.
A day of play came with silence and despair,
as she fell,
summoned by the deep well.

# Time Will Tell

Whether a touch will be real,
whether a day will turn
into a night.
Through many things will be wrong,
many will be right.
Many embraces will lapse in time,
true moments will stand
in the realness, like a blink of an eye.
Time will tell, for there will be
no why's
only you and I.
Our minds will be clear
and our hearts sincere.
On a path that few have chosen,
you and me.
There may be bumps in the path,
but we shall not fear,
as we whisper love into the daylight,
just you wait and see, year to year.
Time will tell when our hearts will repel
into the depths of our sea.
Our goldeness will rise up,
like a refreshing summer breeze
that soars abundantly
beneath the rare trees.
Time will tell,
yes time will tell,
just you and me.

## Gone, Just Gone

Beneath my yesterdays
went tomorrows new dawn,
as mornings breathe a summer's dew.
Midnight sparkles so clear
it rings tears of a sky so blue
that never came that day.
Drifting on a dream
that falls beneath distant echoes,
behind distant walls
that drip lifeless moments.
One desires romantic desires beyond the darkened night.
Hardened reflections pace
within a mind and wayward memories
never see the passages of light.

## An Article of Death

Could thy soul run like a winter's wind?
With only stillness and darkness as my friend?
Hollowed bones within one's self,
no glamour, no materialistic wealth,
and no gold.
Silenced in memories of a new dawn,
whisked away to a world beyond.
Now measured by thy deeds, some good,
so many wrongs,
with ceremonial tears, through ceremonial songs.
Watchful eyes, they do compare
to busy little bees, do beware.
Young hearts mourn
with distant nightmares.
Frantic moves
to thy soul be true,
tearless moments so bitter
and cruel.
Remember, trees of a forest
do fall down,
back to thy mother,
back to thy ground.

## Oh My Marie, Part I

My heart, my love to thee
my truth, my sorrow
Oh My Marie.

Her love so true that awaits for me,
beyond the silence
of a new day
beneath the depths of the sea,
Oh My Marie.

My heart, my love, to thee
upon a glance she came to me—
forbidden passion, my true melody.
Through channeled spirits
for I decree,
for God Almighty
sent her to me
from a wayward galaxy,
Oh My Marie.

Sweeter than honey, so sweet to me,
she went a-dancing on the great ship Liberty
down by the sea that awaits for me,
Oh My Marie.

Her vision, her laughter
twas true joy to me
reflected moments from a mirrored sea.
My heart, my true liberty
that awaits for me, My Marie.

She went a-dancing down by the sea
with her joy and laughter
on a wayward spree,
my true heart yearns for thee,
Oh My Marie.

*Lions At The Gate* | 53

# Oh My Marie, Part II

My heart yearns for thee,
Oh My Marie,
taken from me, My Marie.

Gone beyond the oceans, beyond the sea,
beyond the mountains, through the valleys
and beyond the prairies.

Through the river abroad and quiet trees,
beneath the sandstorms of afar
beyond the galaxies, beyond the midnight stars.

My heart belongs only to thee,
Oh My Marie,
taken from me on a wayward spree
beyond the mountains, beyond the sea
that waits for me, My Marie.

A songbird sings a little tweedle dee
for My beloved Marie.
She went away, to a better day.
My heart yearns for you and me,
every twelfth hour of a day
for My Marie.

Nor lock, nor key chained to My Marie.
Many voyages across the sea
in search of My Marie.
Through lands of love and sweet melodies
lost in My Marie.

As they stop and stare
no love could compare,
only my love for thee,
My Marie.

# Echoes in the Galleys

Shutters pit and pat—
the nightly calls
Silent chatter
through silent halls
Shouting out
within one's mind.
Faded shadows
begin to unwind.
Murmured secrets
do unfold.
Wear souls
shackled to the frosty cold.
Hound howl to one's delight.
Shaded windows of a darkened night.
Echoes in the galleys and spirits fly,
through chanting voices in the sky.
Wicker broomsticks soar to a degree
with tears beneath the sea.
stone plotted memories on a quiet hill,
sleeping reflections and zeal.
Bountiful harvests stand tall and wide.
Predators swing from side to side,
with dart-like moves to soon subside.
Beyond a shadow, one moon appears,
one master of the night, from year to year.

# My Certainty—Love

Lips so divine,
of a true melody.
My heart sings of touches so rare,
subtle kisses beneath
a sorrowed willow tree.
To see beyond the still air.

Your seas are calm at times
with golden embraces that glow within,
true melodies that seem to rhyme
with whirled sensations that flow through my mind.

Caressed through a gentle reprieve,
beyond the silent strokes, "I declare"
and wondrous pieces
flow out to my sea,
through wind and rain and fresh air.

Vowed through my eternity,
bound to a place
forever more
within a destiny that awaits for me,
although my spirit yearns
behind my door of life.

## Shanties Down By the Railroad Tracks

Times are different here,
lonely tears fall well into
an eternal past.
Every day time reaches
into an unforgiven yesterday,
and broken wills that last
beyond tomorrow.
Beneath shattered frowns,
through hidden laughter,
turned upside down, down
down, one broken crown.
The train whistles blow
by and by, though hope
has gone its way
and bitterness begins to play
as the little children cry.
Who will see beyond the riches and lies?
The clouds of doom hover in the sky.
For who has forgotten,
the shanties by the railroad tracks?

## Mercy On Me

Sounding fears hurt so dear
jagged thoughts
wrap around me.
Haunted passages flash
beyond my moment of time.
Are they real?
For who will haunt my lonely sea this day,
Mercy, Mercy, Me.

## Oh What a Web She Spins

Through heartaches, pain, and lustful deceit,
saddened turns on her webbed, lonely streets.
She spins a web of no retreat.

Entangled hearts, bodies and souls—
a struggle for young and old,
Piercing touches and dangerous thrills,
trusting for more, now, one weakened will.

Struggling to survive with just one catch,
searching for her mate, but never a match.
She spins her web, "Oh what a mighty web,"
Dancing pleasure
in a deadly bed.

## Savannah

Savannah was her name
no fortune, nor fame,
her eyes were like a day of rain.
I knew not from whence she came,
a dancer from the port of Spain?
She danced so well, like a wind-swept sail.
Savannah was her name,
no riches, nor fame.
She danced in the night, she danced in the day.
She danced her heart away.
She said, "She danced of days gone by."
Moments of heartache, she knew not why.

# Young Love, Part I

My world is new, with so many things to do
I would like to be a king and live in a castle
to have my queen with one gold tassel
to be caressed in the day and on moonlit nights
dine near roses and candlelight
take a trip to Paris and watch them play
have songs so sweet come my way
take a ride on the trains of love
fly to lands from high above
land in paradise and see wondrous sites
see mountain peaks from enormous heights
dance to music that songbirds make
fall asleep in love and never awake.

## One More Night With You

We set our sails among the many seas,
within the waves of life and the Caribbean breeze.
Through paradise and romantic touches of gold,
gallant embraces, oh so bold.
Dancing beneath the starry nights,
providing glances of volcano lights.
Deep in the Amazon, we took a ride,
romantic campfires, side by side.
Walk on sandy beaches and watch the waves rush in,
falling stars and caressing winds.
My heart skips a beat as our time is near,
duty, plus honor, and quiet fears.

# We Only Have Today

We dream of far away places, fortune and fame
secret treasures, not yet to be claimed.
A knight in shining armor to take us away,
to paradise, beyond the Milky Way.
We dream of silver and gold,
never dying and never growing old.
We teach our children the best we can—
sharing moments with a childhood friend.
Talking to our God, from season to season.
We stop and stare, at days gone by,
review our past and wonder why?
Nothing left to do, nothing left to say
for we only have today.

## Torn at the Seams

Within the depths of one's soul
    reality and fantasy take their toll.
With silent tears running down my face,
torn emotions run at a hurried pace.
Heart-wrenching choices and painful decisions to make.
One glance at your picture, I begin to shake.
Remembrance of days and caressing nights,
candle lit dinners and gondola sights.
Hurried decisions and rushed fights
a cross between rage and passion, the two begin to fight.
One for you, one for her, as a new day begins.
Over and over darkness surrounds the days,
vows are broken in misguided ways.
Reality has spoken in darkened dreams,
Torn, oh yea! Torn at the seams.

## Warriors of the Night

Beneath the hollow echoes which ring
in a distant ear,
quietness shivers and shakes
the true fears of Life.
Through distant mountains that rumble
its truth to bear, beyond the silent truth there.
Gallant warriors of the night roam
beneath the troubled strife,
silent cries reach between the thin air
that calls the bold, the few and the sincere.
Bound on a journey
to bring forth the past
into a light that separates darkness
to truth so rare.
Though clouds may soar
inside a lonely soul—do they last?
Last until tomorrow or will they
always be there,
within warriors of the night,
who bring forth truth
to the light.
Will we find our way to the true light?

## Blind Fears

Beyond a moment that only a
shattered mind will bring
a deceptable truth, the unforeseen,
as casting doubt, a lonely separation
of one's faith into that reality of life.
Beyond the loneliness of one's soul
in need of repair from a lost
direction, beneath the darkness
of pain and strife.
Beyond inner voices that are carriers
of messages that give comfort
through darkened moments
flaring their hardness,
 bitterness and self-inflicted
tears into the realness
of true light.
Through many trials and shaken dreams
that run like weary ripples
from a lonely sea,
that disappear into
the sands of a distant shore,
like inner fears that drift away
into a moment that shall be now more.

## An Enchanted Night

The winds that came a roaring in
across the sandy night
as the night predators
began their flight.
Though the midnight glittered
its quiet delight,
beyond frantic candles that swayed
through a distant light.
Beneath workers that pound
their tiring plight
while lovers caress beneath the starlight.

# IV.

## *Religion*

# Hungered Thy Flesh

Thy mind was lost and still
thy hungered thy flesh.

Thy heart was lonely and mournful
tears and darkness reached into
my light of day,
my eyes became unfocused
still thy hungered thy flesh.

Thy tears fall down onto the ground,
still, thy hungered thy flesh.

Thy soul weeps, within my sleep,
as distant echoes begin to creep.

Thy thirst unquenched with joy or hope
and still thy hungered thy flesh.

Thy hungered thy flesh.

## Angels Among Us

The glowing light of a new dawn
true hope is only a dream away,
beyond the mist of a misguided way.
Through quiet galleys that echo
one true heart, to be or not to be.
Angels stand at the gate of life
or death.
Although they transport the soul
of one's eternal being,
through their saddened strife.
Upon this journey that must stand still
beyond the mountains that rumble
like fallen windmills
like musical harps that
sing a true melody.
True guardians of the light,
that is abundantly true
yet silent to life, for me and you.

## The Rock of Time

My rock, that withstands all test of Time
beneath the strength and through your sighs
that lie within me, beyond the depths of the sea.
Thou stillness and silence is your loving way.
Bound to a glory, bound to a child's silent day,
that stands so tall and yet humble and free.
Through wars of teared moments, my blanket
and my sorrow to be.
My rock of laughter in my joyful spree.
My truth, my freedom and my true liberty,
my rock of dreams, love and my true destiny.
Beneath a quiet willow tree, that dangles its true serenity
beyond the silent decree.

## Destroying the King

We're hunting today, in search of the King,
looking beneath the shady bushes
upon valleys and hills.
Silent bells ring
inside a moment that creeps a slumbered zeal.

We're looking through the bottomless pits,
they say he's there, with hope,
laughter and eternal joy.
He's always about his wits.

We're hunting to destroy the King,
with spirited pleasure
and an altered mind.

Seeking darkened pleasure that never pleases
stories of tears, broken years, and echoed fears
 that change a peaceful heart
and a peaceful mind.

We're hunting to destroy the King
with shameful deeds that never please.

With worldly flangs and flings
idols of worship
and fancy things,
selfish blunder that breaks the heart.

We're hunting to destroy the King,
with arrows that pierce, cold through his soul,
with lustful harvest and worldly things,
smiles and frowns turned upside down.

Lost in the bitter darkness and dreams that turn into
nightmares, with in the inner soul.
We're hunting today to destroy the King
and the King is hunting for us
to give us eternal Life.
The body is the temple.

# The Hunter

He hunts the day
to devour his prey.
For he hunts the night, for all
who search for the true light.
Beneath his deceit and pleasure
is sorrow, hurt, and pain.
Beneath the darkness, beneath his rein
he lurks beyond a watchful eye
beneath a dim, shadowy sky.
He bends and breaks true hearts divine,
with shattered tears and shattered minds.
He lurks beneath valleys and fields
of darkened dreams.
Beyond the mountains,
beyond the hills
he envisions death,
destruction
and worldly thrills.
His bed of lust and frantic displays
give everlasting fire for all your days.
He fell from heaven, an angel
with fiery eyes.

## Innocent To Death

Wingless steps towards the chamberless court,
Nowhere to run, nor to hide,
ye must repent.
Represented by life, represented by death.
Patiently awaiting the mighty call,
behold the mighty gavel
that stands so tall.

## A Kid's Prayer to God

God, if you can hear me
on this beautiful starry night,
I pray that Mommy and Daddy
will always hold me tight.

God, can you have Uncle Bobby's cough go away?
Maybe he'll feel lots better when he comes to pick me up today.
God will you let my sister walk
without those awful crutches she has to keep by her bedside?
I want to let her take my big red bike for a ride.

God, if I'm not asking too much,
there's a little boy and girl that live next door,
their Mother and Father
have gone off to that big bad War.
Can you bring them home from those troubled shores?

God, I know that we must say our prayers
before we eat and before we go to bed at night
and learn wrong from right.

God, I know you sent your only son to save us
from all our sins, but could you find a place
for the Homeless to come in
out of the cold?

God, we love you with all of our hearts
so could you bring all the families together that are apart?

I know I'm taking up a lot of your precious time,
but why do people have tears in their eyes?
Why does a baby grow up to cry?

Oh God, I read the Bible each and every day
to keep me going the right way.
Last, but not least, God I hope I didn't take a lot of your time,
but I had to get this off my mind.

## Confessions of a Soul

Through twisted decisions
from a weathered past,
like sifted grains through an hour glass
now silently freed through a word or two,
no longer shackled to the haunted chains of despair.
Beneath the wind, in the darkened air,
boundless tears drip as the morning dew
once many and now few.
Awakened freedom
through reformed confessions.
Through gainful joy and heightened expressions.
Beneath the guilt, through all the pain,
replenished growth through thirsty rains.
Once, twice, maybe three times or more
protrude.
Flashes of grandeur beneath the evil war,
heart-filled laughter dances abundantly
and a clear
blossom embraces and reaches out
far and near
through truths and convictions
that trample one's fear.

## Yes I Can

Yes I can and yet I don't
walk through lilies so fresh and new.
Yes I can be still to my heart
and love so real and true.
Born to life that weathers til death
and still remains the same,
into a tomorrow
with each breath
I take only for you.
Yes I can.

## The Pricelessness of Life

Could there be a price for life?
Does life even have a price?
Could it be sorrow, hardships, pain
or is it just strife?
Though weakened morals may cause pain in one's life.
maybe we should think twice
for we have an inner self
that gives us the truth and advice.
For one has only one true life, one heart,
one true soul in repair,
for born of sin, it's always there.
We cause our own hurt and joy
without truth, convictions, and care.
Wisdom is our key when unsettling
times begin to flare.
One moment in time, when darkness
had taken the night,
gone to a silence that's so rare, stillness—
tranquility, calmness, and a distant light in a glare?
For who has been in this moment in time?
The precious, priceless moment there.

LaVergne, TN USA
18 March 2010
176498LV00003B/38/P